HIKING THE
APPALACHIAN TRAIL
– ONE SECTION AT A TIME

*From Georgia to Maine
with 12 States in Between*

By
"Big Bob" Olson

TABLE OF CONTENTS

INTRODUCTION

I'm not sure when the idea to hike the Appalachian Trail (AT) entered my mind, but once there, it kept growing and growing. I have always enjoyed the outdoors with many hiking and camping excursions, but had never ventured out on overnight wilderness trips nor hiked any of the AT. Serendipitously, I started to stumble upon articles and books describing the AT and then met hikers that were gracious enough to answer the many questions I had. With the help of a local hiking club and a wonderful Outward Bound trip, I learned the basics of backpacking. I was ready for the great Appalachian Trail.

Now, something you must realize is that the AT is over 2,175 miles long, spanning from Springer Mountain in Georgia to Mt. Katahdin in Maine. It is designed to get hikers up to the highest ridgelines of the Appalachian Mountains and keep them up there as long as it can. I reasoned that I couldn't possibly take off 5 – 6 months to hike the AT in one season and the solution manifested itself to hike it in sections. Okay then, I decided to give it a try for one week to see if it felt right.

Thus I found myself atop Springer Mountain, the southern terminus of the AT, watching a beautiful April sunset and full of extraordinary joy on taking my first hike on this famous trail. I was in good company as spring is the popular starting time for those hikers wanting to trek all the way from Georgia to Maine in one season. I ended up hiking most of Georgia's section on that trip and became fully addicted to hiking all of the AT – one section at a time.

I realize that backpacking is not for everyone, but when I announced to my family & friends that I was going to hike the AT, I got a lot of "What about ___?" questions. Just fill in the blank with shockers like bears, wild boars, skunks, mice, Oh-My-Gosh SNAKES!!!, getting lost, cold, hypothermia, heat, rain, snow, ticks, Lyme disease, injury, blisters, giardia, albino banjo pickers, Eric Rudolf, etc. As my first AT hike approached, I found my imagination running wild and my sleep interrupted by unpleasant hiking images. Only after getting out on the trail, did I then feel perfectly comfortable to be there. In fact, I found backpacking to be a **great stress reducing experience** and I would return home after each hike feeling very refreshed and full of life.

One of the many lessons I learned on my 1-week Outward Bound trip was to do without eating meat, nor drinking coffee or booze. This practice seems to heighten my backpacking experience, plus increases my enjoyment of them afterwards when I get off the trail. During my entire AT journey, I was sorely tempted several times by offers of all three and somehow found the discipline to resist. But, when I finished a section - that was a different story!

It has taken me 158 hiking days spread out over 13 years to section hike all of the AT through wonderfully beautiful sections of **Georgia, North Carolina, Tennessee, Virginia, West Virginia, Maryland, Pennsylvania, New Jersey, New York, Connecticut, Massachusetts, Vermont, New Hampshire, and Maine**. Each state offers its own unique scenery, habitat, and challenges to those willing to hike its section of the AT. The following includes my highlights of hiking the Appalachian Trail by different sections along with an "AT Poem", "Planning Tips", "Some Do's & Don'ts", "Sections Hiked", and a "Backpacking Checklist".

GEORGIA (~75 MILES)

I will always have fond memories of backpacking the Georgia section of the AT in the spring of 1996. Not only was I realizing my dream, but I was also caught up in the camaraderie of the many others on their first AT hike. I found that backpackers are mostly very friendly and quite willing to share knowledge and supplies if needed. I learned many valuable lessons during my one-week hike through Georgia that I still use on backpacking trips.

Be aware that the 75-mile stretch of the AT in Georgia with its many ups and downs is probably the hardest section of the AT below the Mason-Dixon Line. When you get to the top of a mountain, you will have beautiful vistas of the wild Georgia countryside with very little development noted. As you take in the view, though, be sure to look north for the next mountain and accept that you are going to go down and then come back up at the top of it.

My hike actually started at the **Amicalola Falls State Park** visitor center where you can register and weigh your pack. It is then an 8-½ mile trek to Springer Mountain of which the first mile includes a 750-foot elevation rise to the top of Amicalola Falls. It was quite impressive to look directly down the falls along with several other people who were probably staying at the nearby lodge and wondering why I didn't just drive up there.

I spent the night on top of **Springer Mountain** and thoroughly enjoyed watching the sunset, signing the register book, and reading the plaque with Harold Allen's poem that is included at the end of this book. It happened to be a Saturday night so I got to share the mountain with not one, but two Boy Scout troops and many others which really didn't bother me too much since I was just so excited to be there. I also found a small stone to put in my pack and carry on every section of the AT with the intent of placing it on top of Mt. Katahdin, ME some glorious day.

The next day found me hiking north on the great Appalachian Trail. The AT is very well traveled and clearly marked with white blazes which are 2" x 6" rectangular white marks painted intermittently on trees, rocks, etc. After hiking a while, it becomes second nature to recognize the reassuring white blazes to confirm that you are on the AT.

The first few miles were pleasant hiking along mountain streams and through natural cathedrals of hemlock trees, but I was soon to learn my first hard lesson on water management. The day turned out sunny and hot which required extra water to keep myself hydrated. When I reached the **Hawk Mountain Shelter**, I was low on water, but too lazy to hike down to its spring to replenish my supply. Little did I know that I would be hiking the next 6 miles in the hottest part of the afternoon with no water sources available. Suffice it to say, I was very happy and somewhat wiser when I reached **Justus Creek**.

The highest point of the AT in Georgia at 4,461 feet is **Blood Mountain** named after a bloody battle fought there by Native Americans. A stone shelter built by CCC (Civilian Conservation Corps) workers during the 1930's sits on the top of this peak and I was very pleased to spend the night in it since the weather had turned to rain with strong winds. I shared the shelter with several others, which made for a fun atmosphere safe from the outside elements. It was a good idea to get to know some of my fellow hikers as I learned much from them and enjoyed their company intermittently the rest of the week.

At the 31-mile mark, the trail crosses US 19 at **Neels Gap** and goes right through a wonderful oasis called the **Walasi-Yi Center**. After 4 days on the trail, I cannot describe how refreshed I felt after taking a hot shower, getting my clothes washed, and pigging out on ice cream bars. I would have spent the night at their hostel, but all bunk beds were taken. So I carried on and felt pretty good about it later when I found that 1 out of 5 AT hikers bail out by Neels Gap.

The remainder of the Georgia AT section had some very challenging climbs especially at **Unicoi Gap** and **Kelly Knob**, but I was not in a hurry and discovered that a "slow and steady" pace will get you where you want to go. I recall wonderful visions of hiking through an open wooded area full of may apples and indigo buntings; the thrill of reaching the top of an open peak and looking miles in all directions;

hiking through a fairly long stretch of downed trees caused by hurricane Opal; observing flocks of migrating warblers at the different gaps; and setting up camp on mountain tops to watch the sun set, the stars appear, the moon rise, & then the sun to rise again for another great day on the trail.

I finished my first week of the AT on US 76 at **Dick's Creek Gap**, about 8 miles short of the NC border. As much as I enjoyed the trail, it sure was good to head back home and to chow down on a well-deserved cheeseburger, fries, and milkshake along the way. When you have been without, it makes you really appreciate all the many things that we have available to us, but mostly take for granted.

NORTH CAROLINA (~88 MILES)

As soon as the AT crosses into North Carolina, the trail seems to level out and the slopes take on a more gradual grade. Instead of traveling over mountains, the trail mostly follows the contour lines around them.

I chose to start this section of the AT in early November and was to learn another hard trail lesson on the harsher weather conditions at the higher elevations of the mountains. Fortunately, I stayed in shelters on this trip and awoke the first morning to a beautiful sunrise along with ½ inch of fresh snow and cold conditions. The hiking was actually very refreshing and as long as I kept moving, I stayed warm. I spent the second night at **Standing Indian Mountain Shelter** snug in my sleeping bag as another snowstorm hit along with heavy winds and even colder conditions. When I got up the next morning, I decided to bail out and take another trail off the AT to **Rainbow Spring's Campground** where I had parked my car 2 days earlier for a shuttle to the starting point.

When I picked the AT back up again the following spring, I realized what a smart move I had made by bailing out of the cold, snowy conditions at Standing Indian Mountain. I first came to a challenging ½ mile stretch of trail around **Big Butt Mountain** with a narrow trail carved into the side of its steep slope. The deep drop-offs to my right were pretty scary in good weather, but would have been terrifying in snowy conditions. Then came **Albert Mountain** with its ¼ mile scramble up its seemingly vertical boulder-strewn slope. When I reached its summit, I was very thankful for hiking it in good weather.

After hiking many miles in heavily wooded terrain, I reached the top of a mountain with a wonderful open, grassy area. Since the day was sunny, I took the opportunity to shed my pack and shirt and soak up some rays. I discovered that I was on **Siler Bald**, which is the first of many balds that the AT traverses in the southern Appalachians. Balds are mountains with mostly grassy tops that usually offer nice vistas of the surrounding mountains. It is somewhat of a mystery how balds were established during Native American times, but European settlers kept them clear by grazing livestock on them. Now under different management services, the balds are mowed occasionally or allowed to slowly revert to blackberry patches and woodland.

On my fourth day out, I arrived at another wonderful resting area, the **Nantahala Outdoor Center** (NOC) on the famous whitewater

Nantahala River. The NOC has excellent accommodations for hikers, rafters, and other outdoor enthusiasts. I checked in at their hostel, showered up, and then treated myself to a sumptuous dinner at one restaurant and a decadent dessert at another – I deserved it.

The next morning, I chowed down on a lumberjack-size breakfast that I soon regretted as I headed out north on the AT. I was in for a long 8-mile uphill hike that day and felt like I was carrying a lot of extra weight (which I was - in my stomach!). The tough hike was worth it, though, when I finally made it to the top of **Cheoah Bald** and drank in the truly inspiring views of Fontana Lake and the Cheoah/Stecoah mountain ranges.

The last day of this section hike led down into the Little Tennessee River valley and through what I can only describe as a temperate rain forest. Now I am not a flower enthusiast, but during early May on a 2-3 mile stretch just before highway 28 the display of wildflowers was quite spectacular with a kaleidoscope of every color imaginable.

The 88-mile AT stretch through North Carolina ends at **Fontana Dam** with its nice visitor's center complete with tram rides down to view its hydraulic generators. I was very appreciative of its restrooms and took full advantage of the hot showers available there. Just 0.3 miles short of the dam is a nice shelter that is fondly known as the "Fontana Hilton" with pretty views overlooking Fontana Lake. For those continuing on into the **Great Smoky Mountain National Park**, a registration form needs to be filled out at the shelter.

NORTH CAROLINA/TENNESSEE (~220 MILES)

The AT follows the North Carolina/Tennessee border on and off for approximately 220 miles of which the first 70 miles is in the **Great Smoky Mountain National Park** (GSMNP). It is here that the AT reaches its highest elevation peaking at 6,643 feet atop Clingman's Dome. Accept the fact that you are going to do some uphill hiking with an elevation gain of close to one mile, but after the Dome, "it is all downhill from there".

I was surprised when talking to thru-hikers that a lot were glad to put the Smokies behind them. I believe that there are two main reasons for their dislike. First, they were hiking through in the springtime when there is usually more rain and more hikers and second, everyone has to stay in or near shelters. The Smokies have beautiful vistas, but there is not much to see when it is raining and you are up in the clouds. Then when you reach a shelter, you may have to share it with several other hikers along with their damp clothing and supplies.

I chose to backpack the Smokies over two long weekends in September/October and thoroughly enjoyed the hikes with great weather and mostly few shelter mates. As the AT led me up, I was offered higher and better views of the surrounding areas at **Shuckstack Tower**, different fields, and **Rocky Top** (associated with the famous Tennessee song). With the higher elevations, I observed the transition from deciduous to evergreen trees of Fraser firs and red spruce that grow along about 17 miles of AT trail above 5,800 feet. I enjoyed the 360° view from **Clingman's Dome** spiral observation deck along with several other people that had driven to within ½ mile

9

and then "hiked" up there. At these altitudes, you cannot help but notice the many dead Fraser firs that have succumbed to non-native balsam woolly adelgid insects, but beneath these sentinels are a large population of healthy, young firs that will hopefully fair better.

The GSMNP does not allow hunting, which greatly increases populations of most types of wildlife including black bear. Most sightings of bears are just a brief glimpse of something black running away from you as fast as it can. You do need to be smart to not leave your pack unattended and to hang all your food items in a bag on one of their very nice bear lines. Protective fences have been mounted across the front of most shelters as a result of uninformed hikers feeding the "cute" bear, which results in the "not-so-cute-anymore" bear losing its fear of humans and approaching shelters, which then results in the park service having to kill the bear.

The animal that really got my attention in GSMNP was the wild boar. This non-native hog was introduced by hunting clubs years ago and quickly multiplied into a major plant-disturbing nuisance throughout the area. One large boar gave me a couple of deep warning grunts in heavy underbrush just off the trail, which quickened my pace and my heart rate substantially. The GSMNP staff does have a major program in place to eradicate wild boars, but until then, I followed the boar-avoiding advice of not hiking at night.

Beyond **Icewater Spring Shelter**, the AT traverses a 12-mile stretch on high altitude ridgelines with steep drop-offs to each side. The views are spectacular and highlight the grandeur of the Smokies with its vast diversity of flora and fauna.

After leaving GSMNP, the trail leads to perhaps the nicest bald of all on the AT – **Max Patch**. Again, since there is road access, there are usually more people around, which is okay since Max Patch has plenty of room with a lot of beautiful views. I was going to spend the night there, but the threat of a thunderstorm pushed me on to the next shelter.

The following day brought me into the first real trail town on the AT - **Hot Springs, NC**. I thoroughly enjoyed soaking my body in one of their famed hot spring-fed spas while overlooking the French Broad River. Later I dined at one of their fine restaurants and let the roar of the river lull me to sleep at a nearby campsite.

I had great May weather during my 5-day hike from the French Broad River to the **Nolichucky River** near **Erwin, TN**. I fondly remember beautiful views from **Lover's Leap**, a picnic at a pond near Ridge Mill, and sleeping under the stars at **Rich Mountain**, **Camp Creek Bald Fire Tower**, **Frozen Knob**, and **Big Bald**. I reached the **Nolichucky River** on a hot 90° afternoon and finished the hike with a very refreshing swim in its cool waters.

I picked up the trail again with a friend and my dog in early March for what I thought would be a nice spring weekend hiking trip. Again, I learned another hard trail lesson of harsher weather conditions in the mountains. The trek started out innocently at the Nolichucky River, but as the elevation increased, snow started to appear. By the time we reached **Beauty Spot**, a nice bald at elevation 4,437 feet, we were walking in 1-foot of wet slushy snow. It was much slower hiking and at times we had to scout ahead to make sure we were still on the trail. On the positive side, it was very quiet walking in a winter wonderland with observations of many different wild animal tracks and the flushing of a ruffed grouse. The hike up **Unaka Mountain** was tough, but the reward of hiking through its red spruce forest was worth it. The last night of the trip brought temperatures in the low teens which necessitated sleeping with my boots between my dog and myself to keep them from freezing up.

The final AT leg on the NC/TN border leads over **Roan Mountain** and a string of beautiful balds. **Roan Mountain** is famous for its rhododendron gardens that are quite pretty when in full bloom in June. There are remains of an old hotel at the top of Roan Mountain along with some much appreciated restroom facilities.   The AT then traverses a wonderful 12-mile stretch that I rate in my top 5 favorite AT sections with open balds to include **Grassy Ridge** and the **Hump Mountains**.

TENNESSEE (~65 MILES)

The AT cuts west into Tennessee after crossing **US 19E** and then travels north to Virginia. The trail meets up with several creeks that offer some good spots for camping. After the creeks, I remember one tough climb up to the **White Rocks Mountain** fire tower that tired me out so much that I decided to stop at a hostel off nearby **Dennis Cove**

Road. What a good decision! After a hot shower, some family-style meals, and a good night's sleep, I was refreshed and ready to hike on.

I was soon traveling through **Laurel Fork Gorge** with its outstanding waterfall just off the trail. Even on a hot day, it was nice and cool walking along the river bordered on both sides by high canyon walls. This stretch of the AT impressed me so much that I brought my wife back the following year to experience its hiking beauty.

After hiking out of the gorge and across a forested plateau, the AT comes out along the shores of Lake Watauga. The trail follows the southern shore of the lake for 2-3 miles and yes I did take a nice swim to cool off during the heat of the afternoon. The AT then crosses over **Lake Watauga's Dam** before heading up into the Iron Mountains.

Once I reached the top of the Iron Mountain ridgeline, this 30-mile stretch was relatively easy hiking with good views – especially at **Vanderventure Shelter** looking east over Lake Watauga. On June 1st, I was surprised by a brood of a dozen or so ruffed grouse that exploded out in front of me going every which way with the mother grouse trying to lead me away with a faked broken wing. This scene occurred several more times along the way, and each time would startle the heck out of me.

SOUTHERN VIRGINIA (~258 MILES)

Virginia greets the northbound AT hiker with the trail-friendly town of **Damascus**, which opens its arms to the traveler with many shops, eateries, and accommodations. In mid-May, it hosts the popular "Trail

Days" festival with parades, talent shows, vendor booths, and general backpacker camaraderie. In addition to hikers, it is also a cross roads for bicyclers with the Virginia Creeper and Transcontinental Bike Trails traversing right through town.

The AT follows the Virginia Creeper Trail intermittently for several miles along a pleasant mountain creek before diverting off toward the mountains. I spent one night just past Mount Rogers at the very nice **Thomas Knob Shelter** noted for its solar powered privy. The next day I was honored to meet the shelter's namesakes, Mr. and Mrs. Thomas, who were working with a trail crew; he humorously introduced himself as "Mr. Knob".

When I spotted the wild ponies, I knew I was in **Grayson Highlands State Park** with its open fields and rock formations that are reminiscent of Big Sky Montana country. Later, I brought my wife back here for a backpacking trip and we actually had a small herd of cattle pass through our camping area during the night!

It was a real pleasure hiking through Mount Rogers National Recreation Area, which was re-enforced by a stay at their newest shelter near their headquarters. The **Partnership Shelter** is luxurious compared to other shelters with not only a solar powered privy, but also running water and showers. I was lured into my longest hiking day of 25 miles by the description of this shelter **and** being able to order pizzas for delivery at the nearby headquarters - Yum!

Hiking at lower elevations, I encountered my first snakes on the AT. The first was a long black racer stretched across the trail where I couldn't readily see its head or tail; my dog had already stepped over it, so I did the same and we carried on. The next snake was a beautiful timber rattler off to the side of the trail near where we camped at **Crawfish Valley**; it was minding its own business, so we did too, but we did sleep inside our tent that night.

The trail led us up on to Chestnut Ridge with its beautiful flaming azaleas in full blazing bloom. The weather took a change for the worse and we were glad to stay in **Chestnut Knob Shelter** protected from the rain and wind. The next day in clear weather, we enjoyed views overlooking **Burke's Garden** and hiking along Little Wolf and Laurel Creeks.

I hiked the next stretch from I-77 to **Pearisburg, VA** in late August without seeing any other hikers for 24 hours at a time. It was during one of the drought years and water management was a real challenge. It seemed that every other spring had run dry and the ones running were just a trickle. I remember having some trail magic during this time when my water supply was very low and I happened upon a utility line maintenance crew that generously offered me unlimited access to their ice water supply; I left there completely hydrated with water containers full.

Leading into **Pearisburg**, I am told that **Angel's Rest** has a wonderful view of the New River valley, but instead, I got to view the inside of some lovely clouds. The hike up from the New River leads to long open fields along the **VA/WV border** with beautiful vistas overlooking WV. I had a magical time there watching a pair of kestrels hovering into the wind and then dive bombing into the grass for some unknown prey. The next days carried me over a series of mountains and valleys with sightings of the large **Keffer Oak**, remains of old homesteads, billy goats on **Sinking Creek Mountain**, and towering rock formations at **Dragon's Tooth**.

The trail leading toward **Roanoke** is one of my favorite AT sections starting with **McAfee Knob**. I am told that this is the most photographed spot on the AT and that is justifiably so as it offers magnificent views of a lovely valley from atop a flat rock out-cropping. A little further on, the trail follows along the edge of **Tinker Cliffs** for more killer views of the valley. The approach to the **Roanoke** area follows a high rugged ridgeline that offers excellent views to include their water reservoir, which was 28 feet below normal when I went by.

NORTHERN VIRGINIA (~295 MILES)

After Roanoke, the AT leads into the mountains and intermittently follows the Blue Ridge Parkway to Shenandoah National Park. Even in mid-April, the temperatures did get pretty cold with some nights in the teens. I met some interesting backpackers along this stretch with much larger hiking ambitions than just the measly old AT. One started hiking from Key West, FL on January 1st going up the Florida Trail into Alabama's trail system and then over to the AT with plans of taking the AT extension north past Mount Katahdin up to the Gaspe

Peninsula in Quebec, Canada. Another pair of hikers were in the process of trekking cross-country from Virginia Beach, VA all the way to Los Angeles, CA!

My tough hike up to **Apple Orchard Mountain** was rewarded by an open field with an unusual geodesic dome on top. Fortunately, I met a very nice trail maintainer who explained that the dome used to be the main ICBM detection station during the cold war years and included a barracks with 200 troops and even a bowling alley; it is now used by the FAA for airplane tracking. The maintainer also showed me how to identify and pick a plant called ramp, which is like a combination of onion and garlic. That evening at **Thunder Hill Shelter**, I enjoyed some delicious ramp-flavored soup while reading a very funny entry in the register about somebody stealing EPCOT's geodesic dome and placing it on **Apple Orchard Mountain**.

There is a new footbridge over the **James River** built on old railroad piers that allows for a nice up-close view of this historic river. Then as you are heading north, the overlooks from the Rocky Rows give quite good vistas of the river valley. Later on, I almost stayed at **Punchbowl Shelter** with its neat pond teeming with salamanders, polliwogs, and minnows, but a large group pulled in and I decided to pull out.

After passing by Lynchburg's reservoir at **Pedlar Lake**, I came upon the remains of old homesteads along Brown Mountain Creek with good interpretive signs describing how freed slaves had set up a community there after the Civil War. I then hiked another nice stretch of balds before reaching the lookouts at **Spy Rock** and **Priest Mountain**. The clouds moved in when I hiked the rugged **Three Ridges** giving me a very uplifting, surreal hiking experience. The last trail section before **I-64 at Rockfish Gap** included the very popular day hiking area of **Humpback Mountain** with its challenging rocks.

The AT traverses 107 hiker-friendly miles through **Shenandoah National Park** (SNP) and actually crosses the Skyline Drive 45 times. The prohibition of hunting and the narrowness of the park bring about the best wildlife viewing along the southern AT. The hiker needs to keep his camera at the ready not only for the great vistas, but also natural settings of the many approachable deer. Black Bear observations are frequent, but my personal favorite was a sighting of three wild bobcats!

SNP calls their shelters "huts" for some reason and I was glad to stay in them the first two nights since it was rainy. On the third day, it was very nice to stop at **Loft Mountain camp store** to freshen up and dry some wet clothes at their laundromat. I also took advantage of SNP's three good restaurants along the way for sumptuous lunches and killer blackberry shakes.

I remember hiking through some unique rock fields with no vegetation that seemed to be formed by avalanches. I especially liked the views from **Little Stoney Man Cliffs** and **Mary's Rock**. Upon reaching Mary's Rest in the afternoon, I enjoyed some serious sun napping on its rocks. I awoke feeling hungry, so I cooked a nice supper and watched the sunset over the Shenandoah Valley. Since no one else was around, it seemed natural to just unfold my bedroll there and sleep under the stars. I had a good view of the northern skies and thoroughly enjoyed the age-old observation of the Big Dipper and Cassiopeia seemingly revolving around the North Star during the night.

The day after leaving SNP, I had another extraordinary wildflower experience while walking through **G. R. Thompson Wildlife Management Area**. Luckily, it was late April and the trilliums were in full bloom and lavishly carpeted miles and miles of the forest floor.

While hiking through northern Virginia, there is ample evidence of old home sites. I was able to pick several apples along the way from orchards mixed in the hardwoods and walked along lots of old stone walls. One stone wall just before **US 50**, was reportedly surveyed by a young George Washington.

Virginia contains more than one fourth of the Appalachian Trail at 550+ miles, which took me a total of 40 days to hike. I would rate most of this section as moderate, but there are some strenuous stretches including the famous 18-mile roller coasters to test you before leaving this great state. Again, the "slow and steady approach" worked just fine for me along with the awaited reward of staying at a nice hostel afterward.

WEST VIRGINIA/MARYLAND (~43 MILES)

West Virginia has only 3 miles of the AT within its borders, but has the honor of hosting the Appalachian Trail Conservancy (ATC) headquarters at **Harper's Ferry**. It is quite exciting hiking down to **Harper's Ferry** with the trail going alongside old Civil War entrenchments and crossing the **Shenandoah River**. My first visit was to the ATC headquarters where the friendly staff took my picture for their photo album and in general made me feel very much at home.

I spent an enjoyable afternoon exploring around **Harper's Ferry**, which is really a National Historic Park situated at the juncture of the **Shenandoah and Potomac Rivers**. I had a lot of fun at the balanced Jefferson Rock taking pictures with a group of 8th graders on a school field trip. Later, I tried to enter a quaint-looking general store for supplies, but soon realized that it was just a mock-up building reconstructed to match the days of John Brown's famous raid in 1859. I did enjoy a nice lunch there and was able to get some supplies, but mostly there are not many other hiker services there.

The bridge across the **Potomac River** led me into Maryland and on to the amazing **C&O Canal Towpath**. This towpath is actually a park that follows along the Maryland side of the Potomac River for 180 miles and is conducive for walkers and bicyclers to travel along its way. The AT follows the towpath downstream for three miles before ascending to **Weverton Cliffs** with beautiful views overlooking the Potomac River.

My first full day in Maryland happened to coincide with a neat event sponsored by local hiking clubs for participants to traverse all of the 40-mile Maryland AT section in one day. As I was heading north, I was surprised to see 106 participants jogging, walking, and later in the day, plodding south along the trail.

The Maryland section of the AT has many areas of interest along the way to include Civil War sites at **Gathland State Park** and **Reno Monument**. There are also great vistas at **Washington Monument State Park**, **Annapolis Rocks**, and **Black Rock Cliffs**. This section finishes up at **Pen Mar County Park** where the nearby community locals can gather in the evenings to watch the sunset at its nice pavilion. From there, it is just a short walk to the famous **Mason-Dixon Line**.

PENNSYLVANIA (~230 MILES)

While hiking the southern Appalachian Trail, I had been warned numerous times by southbound hikers about all the rocks that you would encounter on the Pennsylvania section of the AT. Therefore, after crossing the **Mason-Dixon Line**, I was pleasantly surprised to encounter relatively easy terrain during the first week of hiking. In mid-June, the mountain laurel was in full bloom and there were many stretches of beautiful laurel corridors that felt like you were walking through a cathedral. The stop at **Pine Grove State Park** featured an old smelting furnace with interesting illustrations and also the Iron Masters Mansion hostel, which has a secret room that was used as a resting station along the old Underground Railroad. This park is near the half way point of the AT and they have a tradition there about joining the "half-gallon club", which involves eating a half-gallon of ice cream. I just had a pint to eat and then cleaned up at a spigot, put on fresh clothes, and continued north.

The first day of summer, 6/21, is also known as "Hike Naked Day". I met up with a southbound Wilderness Youth Group that told me about their encounter with some "wildlife" observed from someone ahead of me that was hiking naked; apparently it wasn't a very pretty sight. That evening I camped in a somewhat secluded area by a stream – so I hiked around naked for 5-10 minutes – I think I heard some squirrels saying "put it on, put it on".

The weather was most pleasant as I hiked through the quaint trail town of **Boiling Springs** with its beautiful spring-fed lake that feeds into another old iron smelting operation. The staff at the ATC regional office there was most helpful in arranging shuttle service for me. The next day brought me through a relatively flat stretch of trail as it skirts around **Harrisburg** following the borders of open farm fields. Later, the trail into **Duncannon** offered beautiful views overlooking the Susquehanna River. In **Duncannon**, I spent the night at the Doyle Hotel that has seen better days, but is perfect for hikers with inexpensive rooms and hot showers.

On my drive home from this section, I stopped by Gettysburg for a couple hour tour of this famous battle site. Then I continued on the road bringing with me some very pleasant hiking memories, but also something more insidious. After a couple of days at home, I noticed a classic bull's-eye mark on my arm. I had it checked out at the doctor's, and sure enough I had contracted Lyme disease from a probable, unseen deer tick. Since I caught it early, I just took a round of antibiotics to be rid of it before it progressed to my joints and then nerves.

On my next section hike after Duncannon, I started to hit some stretches with lots of rocks and poison ivy. One day I pushed myself with a 22-mile hike to get to a shelter since rain was threatening, but never came. Still it was nice to accomplish and also nice to sleep ~12 hours. It's amazing how much sleep one gets on the trail. When it gets dark, you go to sleep and when it gets light, you wake up. There is something very simple and yet very profound in that.

I camped at some interesting places to include **Fort Dietrich Snyder Mark** where I got water from the same spring that a Colonel Benjamin Franklin did in 1755. The stay at **Port Clinton** was OK, but could have been more trail friendly. The highlight was probably the **Pinnacle Rock** outcrop with killer views of Allentown and the rest of Pennsylvania's AT ridgeline to NJ. That night I just unrolled my bedroll and viewed a light show of the cities beneath the stars. The last stop in PA was at the friendly trail town of **Delaware Water Gap** with nice restaurants and a great church hostel to spend the night.

During its northern half of the AT, Pennsylvania lives up to its trail name of "Rocksylvania. Apparently the southward march of the glaciers during the ice age, ended in northern PA and deposited an enormous amount of rocks. The trail was especially tough between **Wind Gap** & **Wolf Rocks**. There was also the infamous 1-mile scramble out of **Lehigh Gap** over huge boulders, which is then followed by a 4-mile stretch with very little vegetation due to the fallout from an old Zinc smelting plant upwind on the Lehigh River – very weird terrain! For every section of rocky trail, though, there were two sections of good trail, but it's only the rocky sections that you hear about. After a while, you do get used to the rocks in terms of striding from one landing spot to another. It's best to master this rocky terrain in PA since you will be seeing much more of it as you travel north especially in NH & ME.

NEW JERSEY (~72 MILES)

Welcome to New Jersey - 7 states down and 7 to go! I used to think of New Jersey as a suburb of New York City and Philadelphia with lots of buildings and industry, but the 72 mile stretch of the AT in northwest NJ, showed me its wild side. The glaciers had also visited NJ during the ice age and deposited a fair amount of rocks, but also formed many glacial lakes.

It was a hot, sunny day for me walking over the **Delaware River** and then hiking up to the AT's southern-most glacial lake of **Sunfish Pond**; it was most pleasant to soak my tired feet in its cold waters. I spent one night at **Catfish Fire Tower** and tried sleeping under the stars without a tent. During the night, I was awakened by something crawling around in my sleeping bag; it took a while to find the culprit – a caterpillar – and send it flying. Then, even though it wasn't forecast to rain, it did – so I had to put my tent up hurriedly in the wee hours.

I had a nice hike through **High Point State Park** with its obelisk monument (like Washington's) on the highest elevation point of NJ (1803 feet). The **Wallkill Valley** was a pleasure to walk with long stretches of boardwalk over swamps, bogs, and streams; its National Wildlife Reserve had lots of water birds to observe including an immature bald eagle.

NEW YORK (~88 MILES)

The first half of New York's AT, is actually rather rugged with lots of hard ups & downs to include some vertical mountain climbing stretches and long uphill treks at **West** and **Bear Mountains**. There was one tricky spot called the "**Lemon Squeezer**", where I had to remove my pack to get through. The addition of light rain didn't help and I was quite happy to have my trekking poles along to prevent slipping falls. It was good to stay in dry shelters along the way, but one night we were joined by a Boy Scout troop **and** an adventure group that camped nearby. Fortunately, they had hiked ~5 miles that day and went to bed at ~9 PM.

It was a nice, sunny afternoon when I reached the top of **Bear Mountain** to be greeted by lots of day visitors including a bunch of bikers. There were beautiful views of the **Hudson River** and the skyline of New York City on the horizon. After hiking over the **Hudson River**, the terrain became much easier with the trail following the contours more. I enjoyed camping with an overview of **Canopus Lake** and taking sun naps during my mid-day rest stops. There were several road crossings to include a stop off **NY 52** for a great sandwich at a local deli and then on **County Road 20** to admire **Dover Oak**; there was even a railroad crossing where the AT had its own commuter train stop!

CONNECTICUT (~52 MILES)

I had been hiking for 2 weeks when I rolled into **Kent, Connecticut**. During the previous days, I had been envisioning all of the goodies that I was missing and thus enjoyed a big, juicy cheeseburger, fries, milk shake, and 3 root beers at a local café for lunch. That evening, after a long, long hot shower, I enjoyed thick meat-lovers pizza and a cold beer or five. I figured that I deserved it as my metabolism had kicked into high gear and easily burned up the calories taken in.

I started my next 2-week hiking session the following year at **Kent** where I would finish the CT stretch of the AT and progress to Killington, VT. During the first few miles of the trail, I had several discussions with myself about getting into better shape **before** the backpacking trip. Much of the trail follows along the mighty Housatonic River where I had good views of the Great Falls near the aptly named **Falls Village** and enjoyed watching a female common merganser with about a dozen younglings on her back. The **Hang Glider View** overlook allowed observation of the scenic countryside to include a classic 1.5 mile racecourse. Before leaving CT, I rented a room for the night in the neat town of **Salisbury**, where the landlady attracted wild gray foxes to a feeding station in her backyard.

MASSACHUSETTS (~90 MILES)

The first 8 miles in MA was pretty tough, but very beautiful through the **Sage's Ravine** area. I was able to meet up with some Boston family members at **Guilder Pond** for a very nice picnic. After saying my good byes, I hiked off at a fairly fast clip in order to reach a good campsite before dark. Suddenly, I had to hit the brakes hard as I came upon a large timber rattlesnake (~3' long) stretched completely across the trail with his rattle just a-shaking. After admiring its beauty and taking pictures, I wanted it to move along so that I could continue on. I didn't want to throw pebbles, but then found a bag of grapes in my pocket from my picnic lunch – after several throws, I finally hit the snake in the head with a grape and it moved on.

The next day brought me to lower elevations (below 1000 feet) and into mosquito territory. I had to keep walking at a brisk pace to keep them at bay and was wondering if I would be able to stop for a rest. Fortunately, I came upon a day hiker that provided some trail magic by giving me a container of insect spray – heavy on DEET. That evening, I set up my tent in record time and dove inside to escape the mosquito hordes.

I thoroughly enjoyed my stay at **Upper Goose Pond Cabin** with its pretty views and its own caretaker, who cooked pasta for dinner and blueberry pancakes for breakfast at no charge. The next day, I pushed myself into a 21 mile hike in order to reach **Dalton** where I discovered that the local inn had the best hot showers anywhere in the world – or so it seemed at the time. I spent my last night in Massachusetts at its highest peak, **Mt. Greylock** (3,491 feet), where I "stealth camped" near the summit by setting my tent up behind some trees.

VERMONT (~149 MILES)

The AT joins Vermont's Long Trail for its first 100 miles in the Green Mountain state. The trail is known as the long, green tunnel as the New England wilderness shows more of itself with a forested landscape and a multitude of beaver ponds, moose scat, porcupines, black flies, etc. As a birdwatcher, I had many avian observations to include a wild turkey with lots of chicks, common loons, and two rare thrushes (Swainson and Bicknell).

My stay in the trail-friendly town of **Manchester Center** included a half day rest where I cleaned up my clothes and myself. My last night on the trail for this 2-week section was at the **Cooper Lodge** shelter near the top of Killington Peak. I did climb up to the top of Killington for a spectacular view of the Green Mountains at the top of the ski slopes there. Since it was drizzling rain, three citizen scientists stayed at the shelter that night and I was able to join them early the next morning for a bird count of Bicknell thrushes that only nest at high elevations.

The following year, I allocated 6 weeks for my last leg of the Appalachian Trail. My strategy was to regain my hiking stamina during the first 2 weeks before tackling the White Mountains of NH and ME that had been described many times by other hikers as being very tough. Two of my nephews joined me (one for 1 day and one for

1 week) starting at **Kent Pond near Killington**. We enjoyed walking the boardwalks over the **Ottauquechee River Flood Plain** before hiking back into the long, green tunnel. We noticed plastic tube systems working their way down hill and originally thought that they were an irrigation system, before finally figuring out that they were sugar maple sap collectors. During one stretch, we missed a turn in the trail and had to back track about ½ mile; the lesson learned (again) was to pay better attention to sticks crossing the trail to designate a turn.

NEW HAMPSHIRE (~165 MILES)

Crossing over the **Connecticut River**, we were welcomed into New Hampshire at the beautiful Dartmouth College town of **Hanover**. After chowing down at an all-you-can-eat pizza parlor, we visited the Dartmouth Outdoor Center and then caught a free bus ride out to a motel – needless to say, the hot shower and freshly laundered clothes were again much appreciated. The next day, I was grateful for New England's wonderful public transportation system as my nephew was able to take a direct bus ride from **Hanover** to Boston's Logan airport for an airplane ride home.

The next couple of days brought me through heavily wooded terrain with moderate difficulty. The presence of many old stone walls gave testimony to settlers from the past. During my stays at shelters, I met several thru-hikers that had been on the trail for 3-4 months already. They were in super hiking condition and ate voraciously to keep from losing even more weight from their already lean bodies. One day, I happened upon a thru-hiker that was having an adverse reaction from a probable yellow jacket bite; fortunately, I had some Benadryl along that he took to reduce the swelling in a fairly short time frame. That night, it was nice to stay at a hostel in **Glen Cliff** and resupply before venturing into the ruggedly beautiful White Mountains. Little did I know at the time, that I would still be carrying most of my week's food supply (~10 lbs.) seven days later.

Welcome to the White Mountains! I first hiked above the timberline on **Mt. Moosilauke** with an elevation gain of 3,400 feet in 3.4 miles – whew! It was neat to see the trees and shrubs get shorter and shorter and then disappear altogether into a rocky, exposed terrain that prompted me to put on my fleece coat and then rain jacket. In order to mark the barren trail, stones are stacked up to form cairns, which act as guide posts for the hiker. I'm sure that the views can be nice on the mountain, but I just got to experience a cold, windy hike through misty clouds. Then as tough as the ascent was, the descent was even harder as the trail followed along the cataracts of Beaver Brook at a very steep angle with several sections having steps and even rebar footholds built into the trail. Did I mention that this was all during a steady drizzle?

Instead of 3-sided shelters, the NH White Mountains have a very nice hut system operated by the Appalachian Mountain Club (AMC) that caters to paying customers with bunk beds (36-96 per hut), hot meals, and oftentimes, entertainment by "The Croo". For AT hikers, they typically have a work-for-stay program that entitles you to meal leftovers and sleeping space on the dining room floor from 9pm to 6am. During my hike through the White Mountains, I stayed at six huts & three hostels – the good news was that I got to eat their nice hot meals – the bad news was that I ended up carrying the extra 10 lbs. of my food supply through the Whites. The first hut encountered was at the scenic **Lonesome Lake** where my first work assignment was to give a talk to the guests that evening and sweep out some bunks.

The next day was another drizzly, cloudy day with winds of 20-30 mph. I did enjoy hiking above the tree line at **Franconia Ridge** as the clouds lifted partially for beautiful views of its unique habitat. This section was followed by **Mt. Garfield** that I didn't appreciate as much with its steep ascent and descent. That day, I pushed on to **Galehead Hut** and got another work-for-stay, which involved a fun Q&A session after supper with the clientele.

NH is definitely the toughest hiking state on the AT especially with wet, rainy conditions. There are lots of rocks (more than PA) plus steep slopes going straight up and down mountains. I can't tell you how many times I had to hoist myself over boulders and work my way down steep verticals. I remember one time when the trail seemed to just disappear with seemingly nowhere to go. Looking around I finally saw a white blaze directing me to go up a very steep section of rocky, rocky trail. When there weren't rocks, the rain turned the trail into a muddy mess with many puddles and some flowing streams. At one brook crossing, my feet slipped out from under me and into the brook I went, which finished the job of drenching me completely. Fortunately,

Zeeland Falls Hut appeared soon thereafter and provided hot soup and a place to drip dry my stuff – I began to realize how remarkably "wash and wear" our bodies are.

I must admit that I was feeling rather down with the steady rain and tough trail conditions. I was bone tired when I finally reached **Crawford Notch** and its AMC Hostel. I felt better the next day after a hot shower, a good night's sleep, and full breakfast. Most of my clothes were still wet and rather dirty, so I headed over to a nearby campground to do laundry and to contemplate things – like, why am I doing this? Then the sun came out and all was much better.

One of my nephews joined me again as we headed north from **Crawford Notch** for some very nice, very pretty hiking. As it turned out, this was the calm before the storm. We made it in to **Mitzpah Spring Hut** too late to get a work-for-stay, so we just paid a nominal fee to stay the night. The notes in my journal that night read "Tomorrow will be a good stretch above the tree line. Hope for good weather."

It was July 4th, when we headed out from **Mitzpah Spring Hut** and found that the weather decided not to cooperate. As soon as we got above tree line, the wind and rain hit us hard with 30-50 mph gusts. It was brutal. After a couple of miles, we stopped for a short break in the lee of a boulder. I told my nephew that this was the toughest hiking conditions that I had ever been in – and then it started to hail! We finally made the 4.7 miles to **Lakes of the Clouds Hut** and signed on for another work-for-stay – it would have been life-threatening if we had to stay outside in the elements. That night we joined the hut crowd in a hilarious Independence Day celebration led by "The Croo" as the weather continued unabated outside.

The next morning, the conditions were even worse with 50-60 mph gusts and 2" of rain predicted. **Mt. Washington**, which was 1.5 miles ahead, had temperatures in the 30's with a wind chill of 18 °F and was predicted to be in the clouds all day long. My nephew and I decided to bail out from the AT with a five mile hike down Tucker's Ravine. This turned out to be a neat section to hike with a waterfall and areas of snow where people were actually snow skiing – remember that this was still July! As we got to lower elevations, the sun came out and it was pleasant with temperatures eventually getting into the 70's – quite a difference from the mountain ridgeline above. When we reached **Pinkham Notch**, my nephew headed back to Boston and I continued on the AT north after temporarily bypassing 15 miles of the trail.

A few days later, I worked my way back for a stay at the Pinkham Notch Hostel and then took a shuttle ride to the top of **Mt. Washington** to reconnect with the AT. What a difference good weather made! I was finally able to hike above the tree line with breath-taking views. I hiked south back to **Lakes of the Clouds Hut** to connect up to where we had bailed out earlier and then hiked back north. The afternoon was mostly clear with great views of the Presidential Mountains of Washington, Jefferson, Adams, and Madison. The Presidential Range forms a "U" around a gulf that a glacier had carved out thousands of years before. There were numerous moraine areas with lots of loose rock to hike over, but who cares about rocks when there are such beautiful views. I rate the Presidential Range as my 2nd most favorite part of the AT, but the weather has to be right. I spent the night at **Madison Spring Hut** for another work-for-stay (dusting the bunk areas and window sills) before heading down to **Pinkham Notch**.

The hike north from **Pinkham Notch** had a tough climb up the **Wildcat Mountains** and then some more stretches of vertical ups and downs over boulders. At Carter Notch Hut, I had a work-for-stay that was really just a stay with the use of a bunk bed since there were only 3 guests there that night. Before leaving NH, I stayed at a hostel and then at **Gentian Pond Shelter** to prepare for Maine.

MAINE (~280 MILES)

The tough, yet wonderful White Mountains continue into Maine for its first 100 miles of the AT. They make you pay physically to hike their trails, but then reward you with stunning views and wildlife encounters in its more remote wilderness. After Stratton, there are frequent stretches along lakes that they call ponds with inviting sandy beaches. There are also at least 10 river fords to negotiate where swift currents came up to my knees and three that reached my upper thighs. Then there is the 100-mile wilderness to traverse before reaching Baxter State Park and the northern terminus of the AT on the mighty Mt. Katahdin.

From the get-go, Maine welcomes you with lots of verticals and boulder fields to hike. I was getting stronger and more used to handling them, but I remember encountering a thru-hiker who was literally crying about how to negotiate a particularly challenging downward vertical stretch. A shelter is called a lean-to in Maine and my stay at **Full Goose Lean-To** was crowded as we rested before tackling the infamous **Mahoosuc Notch** the next day. Some say that this boulder field is the toughest 1-mile stretch of the AT and you know what – I AGREE! It took me a couple of hours to go over and even under boulders. There were 3-4 spots where I had to take my pack off and shove it through small openings and then crawl on after. After the Notch, there came a steep 2-mile climb up the **Mahoosuc Arm**. I felt good about hiking 10 miles that day and rewarded myself with a stay at a nice hostel off **ME 26** in Bethel, ME.

I stayed at **Hall Mountain Lean-To** after hiking over **Baldpate & Wyman Mountains** - Baldpate had beautiful views, but it was windy and cool in the AM and then Wyman had sunny skies in the PM, but there were no views. There was a neat waterfall at **Dunn Notch** with a great view from above that looked down the falls as it descended into a gorge. I started to meet more and more southbound hikers (SOBO's) as they typically start their thru-hikes from Mt. Katahdin in early July after the black flies have dissipated. At **Bemis Mountain Lean-To**, one SOBO hiker from Canada got a fire going, which was nice to sit around whilst sipping on nice, hot green tea.

What a great day of hiking, I had the next day. The sun shone most of the day and the trail was relatively easy. After crossing **ME 17**, I saw my first moose! He was probably using the trail too, but then took off when he saw me. Then I came across a nice sandy beach on **Long Pond** just before **Sabbath Pond Lean-To**. It looked so inviting that I spent an hour swimming, cleaning up (washing and drying out my socks and shirt), and soaking up some rays. At **US 4**, I got a ride to a hostel near **Rangeley** where I cleaned up, resupplied, and then pigged out at a nice Italian Restaurant - yum. It rained all that night into the morning and I almost did a zero day, but the forecast said that the rain would move on, so I moved out and started hiking north. When I reached **Saddleback Mountain**, the clouds parted and the sun came out. I soaked in a few rays up there and had beautiful views of the Rangeley Lakes. The Saddleback Range is now one of my top 5 favorite stretches of the AT with nice, open views of the trail.

After ~4 weeks of backpacking, I was really hitting my hiking stride. Where I used to take several breaks going up a mountain, I was now maintaining a steady pace and then could really cruise on level ground and reasonable declines. At the **Poplar Ridge Lean-To**, I started to calculate what kind of pace that I would have to maintain over my last 13 hiking days to cover the remaining 210 miles to Mt. Katahdin and came up with 16 miles per day – hmmm. That would really be pushing it, so I decided to just take it one day at a time.

I started to develop a routine to wake up with the sun, break camp, and start hiking within 20 minutes. Then after warming up on the trail, I would stop and eat a breakfast bar along with some gorp (mixture of nuts, raisins, pretzels, and anything else that looked good while supplying) along the trail. Considering all the rain, I was fortunate that it mostly occurred at night while I was snug in a Lean-To or hostel. During mid-day, I would usually rest at a mountain vista or perhaps along a pond for a nap while I let my socks air out and my feet dry – most days, the sun would be shining, which was nice.

After sleeping in my tent at **Cracker Cirque Campsite**, I hiked to **ME 27** where I hitched a ride to **Stratton** in the back of a pick-up truck that I shared with a Saint Bernard dog. I enjoyed a sandwich from the deli and bought another one to enjoy later that evening at **Horn's Pond Lean-To**. The next morning, I got up at 5:30 AM with the sunrise, and had a wonderful hike along **Bigelow Range** at 6:30 AM with great views and little wind. While scanning the valley below with my compact binoculars, I spotted a moose foraging along a stream - this vaulted the Bigelows into one of my top 5 favorite AT stretches.

After the **Bigelow Range**, the terrain shifted to the low lands where I hiked an easy 14 miles to **Pierce Pond Lean-To** and then to the **Kennebec River**. I very much appreciated the canoe ferry ride across the river by an ATC employee since the river height can readily rise to 8 feet or more with swift currents due to dam releases. At **US 201**, I hitched a 2-mile ride to Northern Outdoors, which caters to whitewater rafters. They have a terrific setting with a pub brewery, dining area, game room, back deck, and a hot tub! I took a shower, got laundry going, and then soaked in the hot water – it was beautiful! My body and feet actually felt clean. I feasted on a burger and fries and had a great time with other hikers and rafters before retiring to a nice tent cabin on the banks of the Kennebec River.

The trail is definitely easier in the lower elevations of Maine. I hiked 15 miles to **Bald Mountain Brook Lean-To**, but slept in my tent that night to get away from mosquitos and no-see-ums. The next day, I had a monster hike travelling 22 miles to **ME 15** and then hitching into **Monson**. It drizzled all that day, which turned the trail very muddy in many places. There were two interesting fords of the West and East branches of the Piscataquis River where the swift current came up to my knees. Since my hiking shoes, socks, and feet were already soaking, I just hiked across the rivers and kept going. With all the rain and the river crossings, it makes sense to hike with just good, light weight walking shoes. The joke about hiking boots was that the more water proof that they claimed to be, the longer it would take to release the moisture after your feet became water logged.

In **Monson**, I got a bunk at a local hostel and cleaned myself and my clothes. The next morning, I resupplied at the general store with a week's worth of food to carry me through the famous, 100-mile wilderness stretch of the AT, where there are no roads to cross or places to resupply. Over the next couple of days, I encountered lots of PUD's (pointless ups and downs) that with the rainy conditions, I renamed MUD's (meaningless ups and downs). There were numerous stream crossings that were knee to thigh deep but then there was the beautiful **Little Wilson Waterfall** to behold with its stair-step cascade. I slept in late the 3rd morning since it was raining and didn't get hiking until mid-morning. When the sun came out that afternoon, I decided to push on to **White Cap Mountain** to try for a sunset and perhaps a view of Mt. Katahdin – Wrong! A thunderstorm came along and since I couldn't find any tent sites, I boogied down to **Logan Brook Lean-To** before the really hard rainfall hit.

I hiked an easy 20 miles to **Antlers Campsite on Jo-Mary Lake** the next day with long stretches of level ground. There were a couple of hills to climb plus a ford of the **Pleasant River East Branch** that went up to my thighs with fairly swift currents. That was then countered by a great 1 hour stop at **Crawford Pond**'s sandy beach where I swam, dried off wet clothes, and sewed up holes in my shorts' pockets – all done while soaking in some rays on a nice, sunny day. The last few miles became very mosquito-y even with the DEET spray. As I snuggled in my tent that night, I heard the loons calling out and telling me to go to sleep – so I did.

I shouldn't have said that the trail was getting easier since I then hit a real rocky, rooty, muddy section along the **Nahmakanta River** that slowed me down some. I did cruise into another sandy beach on **Nahmakanta Lake** and since the sun was out, I repeated my routine of swimming and washing out my clothes; while they dried out, I proceeded to take a sun nap for a good hour. Then I cruised on to **Wadleigh Stream Lean-To** where I spent the night with 3 other hikers and a teenagers' adventure camp that tented nearby. It started to rain during the night and then really opened up during the wee hours. How many inches of rain fell? I would guess ~3 inches. The tranquil little Wadleigh Stream that I had stepped over yesterday, was now a torrent 12 feet wide. The hike that day was, of course, very sloshy with lots of trail turned into streams and standing water. There were a couple of fords that would normally have been step-overs, but instead, came up knee deep. I did see 3 otters on Rainbow Stream before reaching **Rainbow Lake** where I set up my tent on its shore. I enjoyed a very relaxing meal while sitting on a rock that was jutting out into the lake. As I sipped hot green tea, I contemplated my approach to Baxter State Park and then Mt. Katahdin. Part of me was emotional about being within reach of this major milestone in my life and another part of me just wanted to get it over with and go home.

The next day, I got going by 6 AM and had a beautiful view of Mt. Katahdin from 21 miles away at **Rainbow Ledges** and then again from 15 miles away at the **Abol Bridge** over the **Penobscot River**. While enjoying a sandwich there from Linda's Store, I was greeted by a Baxter State Park employee that registered me into their system. During the last 10 miles to the **Birches Campground**, the Maine weather decided to deliver some more rain – just one more time. There were also 2 more rivers to ford with one of them coming close to my torso. I reported in to the Ranger station, picked up a day pack to use the next day, and then settled into my last Lean-To stay of the hike.

My final day on the Appalachian Trail was one of the most memorable days of my life. I woke up to sunny skies and got hiking by 7:20 AM. There would be a 4000 foot elevation gain during the 5 mile hike up to **Mt. Katahdin**. The first mile was nice along the Katahdin Stream and falls. The trail then started a steady incline for the next 2 miles. There were two ½ mile sections with steep climbs of hand to foot to hand verticals. Then the last 2 miles were wide open above the tree line with gorgeous terrain – this stretch up to Mt. Katahdin would end up being rated my favorite section of the AT. What a feeling of elation in reaching the summit! I was so filled with energy and emotion! I took many pictures on top with incredible views. I also brought out the stone that I had carried all the way from Springer Mountain, GA and placed it on to a cairn at the top of Mt. Katahdin, ME. When I called my wife, I choked up a few times in realizing that I had finally finished the Appalachian Trail – all 2,178.3 miles of it.

I hiked back down and easily hitched a ride to a hostel in Millinocket. After another glorious shower, I went to a local café with several other hikers for some wonderful meat loaf and a few brewski's to celebrate. The next day, I caught a shuttle to Medway and then utilized the great New England public transportation system to get to Boston and then home.

It had been one of the most challenging 6 weeks of my life. My body was certainly stronger and I had lost over 25 pounds (~12.5% of my norm). I had been sending out updates and photos to family, friends, and work associates throughout the trip and came to really appreciate the use of smart phones – what an amazing technology to be able to communicate whilst on top of mountains and in the wilds! It was fun to send out updates and get feedback along the way. Several people said that they felt like they were part of the hike and really looked forward to my emails and pictures. My wife also put pictures into Facebook where lots of others logged in to follow the journey. Then of course, I could call my wife and others like a regular phone. My only regret was not bringing a spare battery and/or charger.

EPILOGUE

I was so content on finishing the great Appalachian Trail and so happy to be at home. As much as I enjoyed the trail, I had been missing my wife & my bed & hot showers & our dogs & all the things that one takes for granted until you have to do without them. My body needed some rest & relaxation after being pushed so hard. During one particularly challenging section of the trail, I remember promising my feet a pedicure if they would get me through all the wet, rocky, and muddy conditions – they did, so I pampered them with a hot wax pedicure along with a full body massage – my whole body deserved it!

When you are out on the trail, you begin to think philosophically. For some reason, I had chosen the hiking of the Appalachian Trail as one of my major life goals and felt that I would discover something about the meaning of life as I traveled it. There were no eureka moments, but I came to realize that the purpose of life is to experience it - and hiking the AT is a great way to experience life in the here and now.

So why do I go backpacking and subject myself to the trail hardships? I do it to get away from the hustle and bustle of the world. I do it for my mind – to reduce stress and to observe new environments. I do it for my body – to get in better shape, to lose a few pounds, to purge meats, booze, and coffee. I do it for my soul – to reconnect with Mother Earth and recharge. The Appalachian Trail is long and tough and when you look at it that way, it is quite overwhelming in its immensity. But when you break it down into sections and then just hike it one step at a time, it gradually unfolds. When you get tired, you rest and then get up and hike some more. The trail is a lot like life with ups & downs, tough obstacles, and easy stretches. It is meant to be experienced. Each step, each mile, each section is an adventure awaiting you. It is amazing all that is out there to be experienced and observed and the Appalachian Trail delivers its fair share.

And my soul? – It just feels right!

AT POEM

Remote for detachment,

Narrow for chosen company,

Winding for leisure,

Lonely for contemplation,

The Appalachian Trail beckons

Not merely north and south,

But upward to the body, mind,

And soul of man.

Harold Allen

PLANNING TIPS

- If you have never backpacked before, it would be a good idea to go out with some experienced hikers for a weekend trip or two to make sure it feels right for you. If your friends don't work out, then check with some local or state hiking clubs for backpacking trips. I chose to go on a challenging Outward Bound trip for my first backpacking experience.

- Equipment-wise, make sure you have a good quality backpack with a comfortable, padded belt that is properly fitted for your hips since that is where most of the pack weight will be borne. Other suggested equipment are sleeping bag, air mattress, pack cover, tent, stove, fuel, pot, utensil, matches, water containers, water filter, trekking poles, small plastic shovel, nylon rope, and first aid kit. Refer to the checklist below for more detail.

- Clothes-wise, make sure you have good quality hiking boots/shoes that are well broken in **before** you start hiking. Over the years, I shifted to lighter weight hiking shoes that were easier to clean up and dry out when hiking in wet conditions. Wear two pairs of socks such as wool socks over polypropylene socks to minimize the chance of blisters. I would also bring along a pair of Crocs (or flip flops) to wear around the camp area to give my feet a break from the hiking shoes. Other clothes suggested are pants with zip-off legs, T-shirts, fleece jacket, hat, bandanna, and rain jacket. Maximize the use of easy-to-dry synthetic fabrics and minimize the use of cotton, as it is hard to dry out when wet; blue jeans are a no-no.

- For food, think simple and dehydrated. For breakfast, I used to boil up water for some instant oatmeal, but found this to be too time consuming. Instead, I would eat a breakfast bar and then throughout the day, snack on a couple of energy bars and a bag of gorp, which is a mixture of whatever looks good in the grocery store to include nuts, M&M's, dried fruit, pretzels, etc. Apples, bagels, and peanut butter also make for nice lunches. For supper, I'd boil up some water for pasta or soup along with perhaps some pita bread; after supper I would use extra boiled water for some hot green tea. Keep your food in a separate, waterproof bag that can be hung away from your pack on a bear line, over a limb, or on a shelter peg.

- Before heading out, load up and weigh your pack. Target pack weight is 15% – 25% of your body weight and certainly no more than 45 pounds. On my first section hike, I started out with a 62-pound pack and got a lot of negative feedback from my body. After several section hikes, I worked my pack weight down to 35-40 pounds, which included 10 lbs. of food that would last ~1 week. It helps to weigh each item that you put in your pack and ask yourself if you really need it; see the lbs.' and ounces" on the checklist below.

- Purchase up-to-date guidebooks and perhaps maps for the area you will be hiking. The Appalachian Trail Conservancy is a good source for the latest materials. I would rip out and carry only the pages needed for the particular section being hiked and then took perverse pleasure in burning or throwing away the pages that covered the trail already hiked.

- The #1 rule in backpacking safety is to let someone know where you will be and when to expect your return. Plan out a day-by-day itinerary for every trip and leave a copy with a responsible person. If possible, check in with a ranger station or local establishment at the point of origin.

- Transportation to and from the trailheads can be a real challenge. It's nice to have a friend drop and pick you up, but too much of this can put a strain on the friendship. The best way is to pay a shuttle service to bring you one way, but this can get expensive at $1.00 - $1.25 per mile (shuttle services can be found in guide books, ranger stations, and word of mouth). If you're hiking in a group, bring two cars and park them at each trailhead. Some trailheads are safe to park a car and some aren't; be sure to check beforehand.

- When hiking the AT, you will need to decide on whether to stay in a tent or in shelters. Shelters are mostly three sided buildings that can sleep 6 - 18 people and are usually spaced 5 – 10 miles apart. If you choose shelters, then you will not need to carry a four-pound tent, but you will need to share the shelter with not only other hikers, but also mice and other creatures. Personally, I usually carry my tent along, but stay in shelters if there is inclement weather. Sometimes, at the beginning of a trip, I will stay at a nice shelter just to meet some fellow hikers.

- Even if you do not stay in shelters, it is a good idea to write something in the shelter registers to let people know you were there. The registers also provide a lot of useful information about the area that you are in plus some very funny and creative writings.

- Be sure to drink plenty of water as you hike, especially on hot, sunny days. I carry at least two quarts of water with me and always know where the next springs will be. I also carry a filter to remove any harmful bacteria that may be in the water. If you want to be double sure of your water supply, you can use iodine or chlorine tablets and/or boil your water.

- Every 3 – 4 days, I try to stop at a hostel or motel to clean up and pamper myself. Most of the hostels along the AT are relatively inexpensive with nice accommodations to include hot showers, a kitchen area, a common room, and your own personal bunk.

SOME DO'S & DON'TS

- Do create a checklist of all your backpacking equipment, clothes, food, etc. and check off each item as you put it in your pack. Don't forget key things like the sleeping air mattress. See below for my checklist.

- Do bring along a journal to write down whatever's on your mind. It is amazing how creative and philosophical you become on the trail away from the hustle and bustle of the everyday world.

- Do talk with other hikers on the trail about the condition of the trail, sights to see, water sources, etc.

- Don't tell others the specifics of where you are going or spending the night especially near road crossings. All of the people that I have met on the trail have been great, but you still need to use common sense to avoid any bad apples.

- Do get trekking poles. They definitely help going uphill, protect your knees going downhill, provide better balance, and can be used in self-defense.

- Don't use cell phones or weather band radios in front of other hikers. Most of them are on the trail to get away from the electronic world.

- Do bring along a bandanna. It has multiple uses to include wiping away sweat, wearing as a head band, handling hot pots, washing off, pre-filtering water, etc.

- Don't bring a dog along if it barks at night, begs for food, and/or is a general nuisance to other hikers. If you do bring a dog, get her/him a pack to carry dog food, bowl, leash, and maybe some of your water, but be sensitive to her/his paw pads as they can be susceptible to cuts and wear. You also need to clean up its poop and make sure it does not mess up water sources. I brought my golden retriever or yellow lab on most AT section hikes and their companionship was very much appreciated by me (and a lot of other hikers).

- Do get a trail name to use on the AT. It is amazing how well trail names and the communication system in general works up and down the trail. My trail name is Big Bob and I have met others like Patella (she had a knee brace), Loon (he was from Minn.), Nothy (Not Over The Hill Yet), Manfree (he just quit the police force), Spokes (he had bicycled across the USA), etc.

- Do hike the Georgia section of the AT in the spring to get a feel for the backpacking spirit of thru-hikers and thru-hiker-wannabes as they first get started. [Author's Note: With the ever increasing number of AT hikers, the ATC is now promoting an alternative plan to start your AT journey at Harper's Ferry, WV. You can hike either south or north and then flip-flop to hike remaining sections.]

- Do keep a list of animals and/or plants that you observe on the AT. I am an avid birdwatcher, but have also honed in my bird listening skills along the trail. So far on the AT, I have identified 123 different species of birds and 20 species of mammals to include the most feared predator on Earth – the human being.

- Don't leave anything behind on the trail. If you pack it in, then be sure to pack it out.

- Do without something while hiking on the trail. Personally, I do not eat meat, nor drink coffee or booze whilst I am out backpacking - it seems to heighten my experience. It also heightens my enjoyment of them afterwards when I finish a backpacking section. [Author's Note: Since completing the AT, I now, do not recommend purging meats as they are a great source of much needed protein - plus jerky tastes so great out on the trail!]

- Don't camp near Boy Scout troops unless they have hiked at least 5 miles that day and are hopefully older Eagle Scouts. I am glad for them getting out in the wilderness, but they can get a little noisy at night.

- Do join the Appalachian Trail Conservancy (appalachiantrail.org) and get subscriptions to magazines such as Backpacker (backpacker.com).

- Do volunteer to help maintain the beautiful Appalachian Trail for future generations to enjoy. Volunteers are coordinated through the ATC and its affiliate-hiking clubs.

SECTIONS HIKED BY BIG BOB

Start of Section		End of Section		Miles Hiked	Days Hiked	Average Miles/Day
Location	Date	Location	Date			
Springer Mtn, GA	4/27/96	Dick's Creek Gap, GA	5/4/96	66.8	7	9.6
Dick's Creek Gap, GA	11/8/96	Standing Indian Shelter, NC	11/10/96	16.5	2	8.3
Standing Indian Shelter, NC	5/3/97	Fontana Dam, NC	5/9/97	79.7	6	13.3
Fontana Dam, NC	9/4/03	Newfound Gap, NC/TN	9/6/03	40.8	2	20.4
Newfound Gap, NC/TN	10/9/03	I-40, NC/TN	10/11/03	32.9	2	16.5
I-40, NC/TN	5/9/98	Erwin, TN	5/16/98	102.2	7	14.6
Erwin, TN	3/5/99	Iron Mountain Gap, TN	3/7/99	19.4	2	9.7
Iron Mountain Gap, TN	5/26/99	Damascus, VA	6/3/99	101.4	8	12.7
Damascus, VA	6/7/99	Atkins, VA	6/11/99	75.3	4	18.8
Atkins, VA	6/13/99	Bastian/Bland, VA	6/16/99	44.4	3	14.8
Bastian/Bland, VA	8/23/99	VA 635	8/27/99	62.1	4	15.5
VA 635	8/30/99	Troutville, VA	9/3/99	74.7	4	18.7
Troutville, VA	4/18/01	US 501 at James River, VA	4/23/01	53.7	5	10.7
US 501 at James River, VA	4/5/02	Rockfish Gap, VA	4/11/02	77.2	6	12.9
Rockfish Gap, VA	9/25/02	Front Royal, VA	10/2/02	107.1	7	15.3
Front Royal, VA	4/28/03	Pen Mar, MD	5/5/03	100.1	7	14.3
Pen Mar, MD	6/18/05	Duncannon, PA	6/24/05	82.9	6	13.8
Duncannon, PA	5/18/06	PA 309	5/25/06	96.6	7	13.8
PA 309	4/19/07	Kent, CT	5/3/07	222.0	14	15.9
Kent, CT	5/21/08	Killington, VT	6/4/08	234.5	14	16.8
Killington, VT	6/21/09	Mt. Katahdin, ME	8/1/09	488.0	41	11.9
			Grand Total	2178.3	158	13.8

BACKPACKING CHECKLIST

(lbs.' ounces")

Equipment	Clothes
___ Backpack (3'5")	___ Rain Jacket
___ Trekking Poles	___ Hat
___ Sleeping Bag/Pillow (3'8")	___ Bandannas
___ Mattress (1'12")	___ Pants/Shorts
___ Tent (3'1")	___ Wool & Polypropylene Socks
___ Stove (14")	___ Hiking Shoes
___ Fuel	___ Crocs
___ Pot/Cup/Utensil (6")	___ Underwear
___ Matches (1")	___ Fleece Jacket
___ Flashlight (2")	___ T-Shirts
___ Binoculars (9")	___ Pillow Case
___ Plastic Shovel & (TP) (3")	___ Change of Clothes for the Car
___ Iodine tablets	
___ Water Containers	
___ Rope/Bag (6")	**Documents**
___ Tooth Paste/Brush (2")	___ Money
___ Hand Sanitizer (2")	___ ATM & VISA
___ Smart Phone/Charger/Battery	___ Driver's License
___ Diary (2")	___ Insurance Card
___ Handbook/Maps (1")	___ AAA Card
___ Pack Cover (8")	
___ Ace Bandage (1")	
___ First Aid Kit/Clippers/Whistle (6")	**Food**
	___ Gorp Mix
	___ Granola Bars
	___ Cheese/Crackers
	___ Meals (Just add hot water)
	___ Green Tea

APPENDIX:
LOCATIONS REFERENCED
BY SECTION

- **<u>Georgia</u>**   <u>Miles from Springer Mtn</u>
  - Amicalola Falls State Park   - 8.5
  - Springer Mountain (Southern Terminus of AT)   0
  - Hawk Mountain Shelter   8
  - Justus Creek   14
  - Blood Mountain Shelter   28
  - Walasi-Yi Center/Neels Gap   31
  - Unicoi Gap   51
  - Kelly Knob   63
  - Dick's Creek Gap (US 76)   68
  - GA/NC Border   76

- **<u>North Carolina</u>**   <u>Miles from Springer Mtn</u>
  - Standing Indian Mountain Shelter   84
  - Big Butt Mountain   95
  - Albert Mountain   98
  - Rainbow Spring's Campground   104
  - Siler Bald   111
  - Nantahala Outdoor Center   135
  - Cheoah Bald   143
  - Fontana Dam/Enter Great Smokey Mountain NP   164

- **<u>North Carolina/Tennessee</u>**   <u>Miles from Springer Mtn</u>
  - Shuckstack Tower   168
  - Rocky Top   182
  - Clingman's Dome   196
  - Icewater Spring Shelter   208
  - I-40/Exit Great Smokey Mountain NP   240
  - Max Patch   252
  - Hot Springs, NC   272

- o Lover's Leap   273
- o Rich Mountain   280
- o Camp Creek Bald Fire Tower   293
- o Frozen Knob   310
- o Big Bald   322
- o Nolichucky River, Erwin, TN   340
- o Beauty Spot   351
- o Unaka Mountain   354
- o Roan Mountain   372
- o Grassy Ridge   376
- o Hump Mountains   382
- o US 19E

- **Tennessee**   Miles from Springer Mtn
  - o White Rocks Mountain   408
  - o Dennis Cove Road   413
  - o Laurel Fork Gorge   414
  - o Lake Watauga Dam   424
  - o Vanderventure Shelter   430
  - o Virginia Border   459

- **Southern Virginia**   Miles from Springer Mtn
  - o Damascus, VA   463
  - o Thomas Knob Shelter   491
  - o Grayson Highlands State Park   496
  - o Partnership Shelter   527
  - o Crawfish Valley   545
  - o Chestnut Knob Shelter   561
  - o Burke's Garden   568
  - o Angel's Rest   623
  - o Pearisburg, VA   626
  - o VA/WV Stretch   633
  - o Keffer Oak   667
  - o Sinking Creek Mountain   674
  - o Dragon's Tooth   690
  - o McAfee Knob   703
  - o Tinker Cliffs   708
  - o Roanoke Area   720

- **Northern Virginia**   Miles from Springer Mtn
  - Apple Orchard Mountain   760
  - Thunder Hill Shelter   761
  - James River   775
  - Punchbowl Shelter   786
  - Pedlar Lake   793
  - Brown Mountain Creek   795
  - Spy Rock   814
  - Priest Mountain   819
  - Three Ridges   829
  - Humpback Mountain   841
  - Rockfish Gap/I-64/ Start Shenandoah NP   853
  - Loft Mountain Camp Store   880
  - Little Stoney Man Cliffs   891
  - Mary's Rock   930
  - G. R. Thompson Wildlife Management Area 972
  - US 50   980

- **West Virginia/Maryland**   Miles from Springer Mtn
  - Shenandoah River   1,012
  - Harper's Ferry, WV   1,013
  - Potomac River/C&O Canal Towpath   1,014
  - Weverton Cliffs   1,018
  - Gathland State Park   1,024
  - Reno Monument   1,030
  - Washington Monument State Park   1,013
  - Annapolis Rocks   1,038
  - Black Rock Cliffs   1,039
  - Pen Mar County Park/Mason-Dixon Line 1,054

- **Pennsylvania**   Miles from Springer Mtn
  - Pine Grove State Park   1,092
  - Boiling Springs, PA   1,112
  - Harrisburg, PA Area   1,121
  - Duncannon, PA   1,137
  - Fort Dietrich Snyder Mark   1,193
  - Port Clinton, PA   1,207
  - Pinnacle Rock   1,217

- o Lehigh Gap   1,247
- o Wind Gap   1,268
- o Wolf Rocks   1,275
- o Delaware Water Gap, PA/Delaware River   1,284
- o Delaware River

• **New Jersey**	Miles from Springer Mtn
o Sunfish Pond	1,290
o Catfish Fire Tower	1,296
o High Point State Park	1,326
o Wallkill Valley	1,338
o New York State Line	1,356

• **New York**	Miles from Springer Mtn
o Lemon Squeezer	1,376
o West Mountain	1,387
o Bear Mountain	1,389
o Hudson River	1,393
o Canopus Lake	1,403
o NY 52	1,423
o Dover Oak/County Road 20	1,435
o Connecticut State Line	1,444

• **Connecticut**	Miles from Springer Mtn
o Kent, CT	1,456
o Falls Village, CT	1,481
o Hang Glider View	1,485
o Salisbury, CT	1,489
o Massachusetts State Line	1,496

• **Massachusetts**	Miles from Springer Mtn
o Sage's Ravine	1,497
o Guilder Pond	1,502
o Upper Goose Pond Cabin	1,538
o Dalton, MA	1,559
o Mt. Greylock	1,576
o Vermont State Line	1,586

- **Vermont**   Miles from Springer Mtn
  - Manchester Center, VT   1,643
  - Cooper Lodge   1,687
  - Kent Pond near Killington, VT   1,698
  - Ottauqueechee River Flood Plain   1,700
  - Connecticut River   1,738

- **New Hampshire**   Miles from Springer Mtn
  - Hanover, NH   1,739
  - Glen Cliff, NH   1,783
  - Mt. Moosilauke   1,788
  - Lonesome Lake Hut   1,805
  - Franconia Ridge   1,810
  - Mt. Garfield   1,818
  - Galehead Hut   1,821
  - Zeeland Falls Hut   1,828
  - Crawford Notch   1,836
  - Mitzpah Spring Hut   1,842
  - Lakes of the Clouds Hut   1,847
  - Mt. Washington   1,849
  - Madison Spring Hut   1,854
  - Pinkham Notch   1,862
  - Wildcat Mountains   1,866
  - Carter Notch Hut   1,868
  - Gentian Pond Shelter   1,895
  - Maine State Line   1,900

- **Maine**   Miles from Springer Mtn
  - Full Goose Lean-To   1,904
  - Mahousuc Notch   1,905
  - Mahousuc Arm   1,906
  - ME 26   1,913
  - Baldpate Mountain   1,917
  - Wyman Mountain   1,927
  - Hall Mountain Lean-To   1,929
  - Dunn Notch   1,935
  - Bemis Mountain Lean-To   1,941
  - ME 17   1,946

- Long Pond — 1,949
- Sabbath Pond Lean-To — 1,950
- US 4/Rangeley, ME — 1,959
- Saddleback Mountain — 1,964
- Poplar Ridge Lean-To — 1,969
- Cracker Cirque Campsite — 1,983
- ME 27/Stratton, ME — 1,990
- Horn's Pond Lean-To — 1,995
- Bigelow Range — 1,999
- Pierce Pond Lean-To — 2,023
- Kennebec River/US 201 — 2,027
- Bald Mountain Brook Lean-To — 2,042
- ME 15/Monson, ME — 2,064
- Little Wilson Waterfall — 2,070
- White Cap Mountain — 2,102
- Logan Brook Lean-To — 2,107
- Pleasant River East Branch — 2,111
- Crawford Pond — 2,116
- Antler's Campground on Jo-Mary Lake — 2,126
- Nahmakanta River — 2,134
- Nahmakanta Lake — 2,137
- Wadleigh Stream Lean-To — 2,140
- Rainbow Lake — 2,150
- Rainbow Ledges — 2,157
- Abol Bridge/Penobscot River — 2,164
- Birches Campground/Ranger's Station — 2,173
- Mt. Katahdin (Northern Terminus of AT) — 2,178